THINK POSITIVE
F E E L G O O D

A W O R K B O O K
TO TRANSFORM YOUR THINKING

New Contact Details:
Tricia Woolfrey
0345 130 0854
tricia@yourempoweredself.co.uk
www.yourempoweredself.co.uk

Tricia Woolfrey

MNLP, DHP, MAPHP, FCIPD

"Most of my worries and fears were being generated in my mind... my negative mind. Using this handbook made me understand what negative thoughts I had. It taught me how to challenge them and, most importantly, how to change them. Thinking positively, I'm able to get on with my life and enjoy any challenges that may face me in my new future."

MW from Middlesex

First published in Great Britain in 2008
by Verity Publishing

2nd Edition
Reprinted 2009

Protected by Karma

A CIP Catalogue of this book is available from the British Library

ISBN 978-0-9558374-1-8

Cover Photo: © istockphoto.com

Printed and bound in
Great Britain by the MPG Books Group,
Bodmin and Kiing's Lynn

DISCLAIMER

Although the author has made every effort to ensure the accuracy and completeness of information contained in this book, no responsibility is assumed for errors, inaccuracies, omissions or inconsistency herein. Any slights of people, places or organisations are unintentional.

The efficacy of the system is in direct proportion to the commitment of the reader to the end result. Persistence and diligence are required.

It is recommended that, in difficult cases, to achieve the very best results, this system be used in conjunction with a competent therapist who can work on the emotiona drivers and on motivation, should these be an issue.

Dedicated to my parents.

With all my love always

**With thanks to all those who helped and
supported me in the creation of this book:**

Tom Woolfrey

Will Bruce

Claudine Bruce

Christine Gladen

Linda Peacock

Jacqueline Burns

Liz Rowlinson

James Munro

Jeanette Hurworth

John Chandler

Sarah Williams

Contents

> Life is a grindstone; whether it grinds you down or polishes you up
> depends on what you do with it.
> **Tom Ross**

Preface

As a hypnotherapist, trainer and coach, I treat a lot of clients with a variety of conditions. I love and am proud of the work I do, but from time to time I find that I have clients for whom I have to think of a new approach. A young woman came to me for for help with self-esteem. She was very bright, had lots of friends and a loving family. Yet her thinking was so negative and so ingrained that she simply wasn't able to enjoy her life. And so I decided to speed up the process of helping her through the treatment by devising this thought-transforming method to help her through her "stuck" periods.

This worked like a dream and helped with the rest of her treatment. She used the sheets I have included in this workbook over the space of several weeks and was able to transform her thinking, to enjoy her successes (she couldn't even see them before) and to enjoy the moment.

I realised that this process could be used by people who weren't able to come and see me. And so this book was written. It is intended to be used on its own, or as part of a coaching or treatment programme.

I intend to create a hypnotherapy CD to accompany the workbook – look out for it at **www.pw-hypnotherapy.co.uk.**

I do hope that you benefit from this as much as my clients have. I would love to have your feedback. Please feel free to email me at **tricia@pw-hypnotherapy.co.uk**

Wishing you success, positivity and all the goodness they bring.

Tricia Woolfrey MNLP, DHP, MAPHP, FCIPD

> You don't find treasure on the surface.
> **Richard Wilkins**

Introduction

For most of us, negative thinking is just something we fall into from time to time, when we are feeling low, and it doesn't take much to snap out of it and adopt our normal happy-go-lucky, life-is-a-breeze style of thinking. For the rest of us, positive thinking seems to be an unattainable ideal which we would but dream about if only we would quit being so downbeat! It can be completely debilitating or simply frustrating – for ourselves and for those we come into contact with. It is never enjoyable and it doesn't make you the easiest person to be around either! It also serves no real, stress-free purpose.

So, this workbook is designed to help you identify your negative thoughts and create more positive, empowering ones, because negative thinking takes so much from you – energy, enthusiasm, good-will, wellbeing and even friendships. In fact, negativity and, in particular, worry is like praying for what you don't want. The only benefit it has is in highlighting problems - and that's only of any use if you actually do something about it. Wallowing in the problem weakens you, disempowers you and diminishes your experience of life.

Let's take Sarah and her beliefs. Beliefs are what we believe as individuals to be true, and act upon as though they are true, rather than what is proven as fact. Sarah's core beliefs were:

I AM	Not good enough
PEOPLE ARE	Difficult
THE WORLD IS	Tough

What kind of life was she leading? Her world was becoming smaller and smaller as she decided to avoid situations which would highlight her lack of worth, steered clear of the "difficult" people who surrounded her and "protected" herself from the world. In reality, the world she inhabited was no different to the world of a "glass half full" person. The difference was in her perceptions. Because she focused on her faults (despite the fact that she was an exceptionally successful businesswoman with a happy marriage), and the problems people caused, her life did in fact feel difficult and tough. But someone else with the same experiences might instead have focused on the fact that, even though life can be tough sometimes, they get through everything, and come out of challenging situations the stronger for them.

Going through life believing, for example, that "people are difficult" causes you to interact with others in a particular way. Perhaps with suspicion, defensiveness or reticence. All of which would cause people to react in a way which would only reinforce your opinion of them. It truly is a self-fulfilling prophecy. This however, is not proof that your opinion is an accurate reflection of reality.

The fact is, that to develop, we need to be able to deal with life's little hurdles. And the big ones too. You've probably heard the saying "there is no failure, only feedback". And that's true. We are always learning and growing, if we choose to. And it **is** a choice. The biggest risk in life is not one of failure but rather one of regret. Regret in not having chosen to give of your best, of not having chosen to have at least tried, of choosing to stay so safe that you didn't live. Negativity can fill your life with regrets because it stops you moving forward. Unless you chose otherwise.

Because Sarah was focusing on all the negatives in her life, that's all she could see and that's all she was attracting.

We create our own reality by how we choose to perceive and react to things and how we behave. Choose your reactions and behaviours and you choose your experience.

It takes some practice to overcome negative thinking. Repetition is key. After all it is by repetition that you negatively programmed yourself. Over time you will find that working through this workbook will loosen your ties to the negative thinking, allowing you to enjoy the benefits of positive thinking. It is a little like a muscle. You have been working your negative-thinking muscle very hard. It's strong! We want to start to develop your positive-thinking muscle so that it becomes the strongest of the two and your new default pattern so that the negative-thinking muscle becomes weak and withered. Repetition is, as they say, the mother of success.

For this reason, there are plenty of blank worksheets for you to practise, practise, practise. There is a motivational quote at the bottom of each page. If you need more worksheets, feel free to photocopy a blank one as many times as you need to.

This workbook is split up into three main parts:

Part I   **Building the Foundations**

- What's in it for you? This section is designed to develop your motivation for change

- Outlines a simple, Ten Step programme to start to re-programme the way you think

- Suggests other simple methods to help break your negative-thinking pattern

- Gives details of numerous negative-thinking patterns, adapted from the work of Dr David Burns who built on the principles of cognitive behavioural therapy developed by Aaron T Beck. These patterns are pretty much fail-safe in terms of helping you feel bad about yourself, others and the world!

- Highlights how a small adjustment in your choice of words can have a significant impact on you

Part II   **The Workbook**

This is the workbook which you use according to the Ten Steps outlined in Part I. Work through each of the steps methodically to help you move from the consequences of your negative thinking towards all the benefits which can be enjoyed through thinking positively. Be thorough, don't skimp. The more you put in, the more you get out. There are a couple of examples for you to get you started. There is also a section titled "How are you doing?" which guides you through any difficulties you may be experiencing with a little added moral support further on in the workbook.

Part III   **Next Steps**

Takes you to the next steps - Beyond the Power of Positive Thought. This is about how you can take your positive thinking to the next level so that you attract what you want in your life.

It also includes a useful resources section which details additional information available to you to help you on your way.

Part III also includes a conclusion to bring it all together.

Have you ever, or do you know of anyone who has, bought an exercise bike to get fit? They put it in their spare bedroom and, apart from a few quick flurries of activity, the bike sits in the corner, gathering dust and its owner no fitter than when they first bought it? So it is with this workbook: to benefit, you have to **use** it, follow the instructions diligently, persistently and you will find that your life and your relationships flourish as a result. Enjoy!

PART 1

What's In It For You?

Before you start, it is a good idea to look at the benefits of positive thinking for you. This will help you to keep motivated through the process. The technique is simple. Using the quadrant below, simply fill in each part according to its title, and look at the merits of change over keeping things as they are. Think about how your life will be different if your thinking is positive. You might want to think in terms of career, relationships, general wellbeing and peace of mind and your day to day experience of life.

List as many as you can. Some examples are given.

BENEFITS OF CHANGE – THINKING POSITIVELY	BENEFITS OF STAYING THE SAME – THINKING NEGATIVELY
ie I will be happier and more confident at work	ie I can say "I knew it" when things go wrong
DISADVANTAGES OF CHANGE – THINKING POSITIVELY	**DISADVANTAGES OF STAYING THE SAME – THINKING NEGATIVELY**
ie It will take effort from me	ie It's a real drain on my energy

If, in doing this exercise, you find that the benefits of negative thinking and the disadvantages of positive thinking are many, then you might want to weight each of the factors in terms of their importance to you to get a better perspective. This should clarify the need for change. If it does not, this simply isn't the time for you to change. You need to really explore your reasons and perhaps work with a qualified counsellor or therapist to help you through this.

Before you decide on that, let's explore some examples of the negatives and put them into perspective:

It will take effort from me

Yes, it will. In the short term. But negative thinking takes a **lot** of energy from you and from others around you. Although making the changes may not be so easy at first, the benefits will be well worth it. Short-term pain – long-term gain!

People may think me weak

There is nothing strong about being negative – it's just a drain on you and others. Being optimistic in our world could in fact be termed a strength – it requires emotional resilience to be able to bounce back and see the good in situations.

People may think me naïve

Where is it written that negative thinking is more realistic than positive thinking? If your tendency is to assume a poor outcome in everything, chances are you are wrong more often than you are right. And whilst optimists may find that they might be wrong from time to time, they will often be right. And their lives will be simpler, richer and happier for their positivity.

I can say "I knew it" when things go wrong

And what do you say when things go right? What would you prefer – to be happy or to be right? It is well known that optimists are happier than pessimists – even if they are wrong some of the time. And pessimists are often wrong themselves. The difference is that they are wrong and unhappy.

My negative thinking protects me

Against what? People who are negative are no safer than those who are positive. To be safe, you need to identify real dangers and take action against them. Avoiding situations simply causes more problems and stops you from growing and developing.

I can use it as an excuse to procrastinate

If we put something off because of fear, it means that it is always looming large ahead of us, like a great big black cloud. As soon as we've done it, it is behind us – done, dusted and you can breathe again and move on, feeling proud.

It gets me attention

What kind of attention do you get from your negativity? Reassurance? This is a sign of insecurity and any sense of security you feel as a result of the reassurance is just is an illusion and feeds the need for continuous reassurance. In reality you are no more secure than anyone who does not have constant reassurance. However, for some people, this kind of attention is the only way they can experience love in their life. If this is the case for you, it is important to start valuing yourself more – to develop a stronger sense of yourself and your worth.

It helps me to be perfect

Perfection is something to move towards – to be the best that we can be and do the best that we can do - but it is not anything we should measure our worth against. The truth is that nobody is perfect. Nobody on this planet, living or dead has achieved perfection because we are all of us works in progress. And that is part of the joy of life – to progress and to learn from our mistakes. For some people their drive for perfection inhibits their ability to enjoy the here and now, and means that what they focus on are the negatives in their lives rather than being able to enjoy all that is good, all that they have achieved and all that they are. To strive for perfection as an absolute is to live a life of disappointment. Much better to **aim** for perfection, accept and learn from mistakes and learn not to take ourselves or our lives quite so seriously.

For the vast majority of people, this exercise will be proof positive that any delay in changing your thinking patterns will be pure folly!

Some Inspirations For You

Victor Frankl (1905-1997)

Victor Frankl was a Jewish psychotherapist who was an inmate in a concentration camp. And, despite the despicable cruelties visited upon him by the Nazis he was able to find meaning in his life. In his book, Man's Search for Meaning – listed as one of the ten most influential books in America (**New York Times**, 1991), he suggests three reactions by fellow inmates to their experience:

1. Shock on initial admission to the camp.
2. Apathy once they became accustomed to life in the camp and where survival is paramount.
3. Depersonalisation, moral deformation, bitterness and disillusionment.

These reactions are not at all surprising, but what Frankl showed in his own response to the cruelty he experienced was the ability to put aside his personal pain in the belief – the knowledge - that everything can be taken from you except the last of human freedoms – the ability to choose your attitude and your thoughts. He said:

"A human being is a deciding being."

If, in the midst of all this pain and cruelty, he was able to keep his spirits high, then we can learn to do so too. By deciding, as did he.

Helen Keller (1880-1968)

Helen Keller lost her sight and hearing at the tender age of 19 months, before she had learned to speak. The American girl was effectively deaf, dumb and blind. Yet, despite these disabilities, she was able to learn to communicate in several different languages, and she became a teacher and a philosopher who was wise beyond her years. Such was her ability to overcome these physical challenges that she was able to go to college and obtain a Bachelor of Arts degree. Whilst at college she began her career in writing, including an essay on Optimism, and became a public speaker through her teacher of many years, Anne Sullivan, travelling the country and earning up to $2000 a week in the early part of the last century.

She is well known for her inspirational quotes, one of which is particularly relevant to this workbook:

"Although the world is full of suffering, it is also full of the overcoming of it."

How true this is. With the right attitude and with determination, we can all overcome whatever suffering besets us in our lives and we can become an inspiration to those around us.

Corrina King (still alive and kicking)

Corrina is a business development manager who attended one of my courses in 2007. She had an inspiring tale to tell which I would like to share with you now. One day she woke up with blood coming out of her ear and her bed soaked with sweat. She had had headaches for a couple of months previously. A CT scan showed a very large mass in her frontal sinus, growing into her brain, about the size of an orange.

At her neurosurgical assessment she was given just two weeks to live. The tumour, whilst benign, was eating into her brain and they were worried that it would cause a seizure that would kill her. She had it removed a few days later.

There was no neurological deficit except for dizziness, but complications followed. She was readmitted to hospital with a low-grade infection seven days later.

She had an incredibly high temperature, she couldn't stand up and she had no orientation ability. In addition, she had a very low pulse rate. The registrar told her "We don't know what's wrong with you. You aren't reacting to the drugs as we would want you to. We would like to operate but it would probably kill you. If your body doesn't respond to the treatment, we will have to operate anyway."

This is when her mind-body connection kicked in. That night as she went to sleep she remembers what she now understands to be an internal inventory and asked every part of her being to work with her body and mind to do what it needed to do to help her get well.

When she woke up the next day and the nurse did the normal observations of temperature, blood pressure, etc, she had returned to normal. The registrar was shocked by the turn of events and asked her what she had done. She responded that her mind had had words with her body. He responded "Well, keep doing it, because it's obviously working".

It was only then that the drugs started to do their work. She was on medication for six months but every day she connected with her body to support the healing.

When she was told it would kill her, she remembered a number of books she had read about positive thinking, dealing with emotional issues and the power of the subconscious mind. So she decided to be positive, to crack a few jokes and to really listen to her body.

Even when everyone around her was negative in their prognosis, she remained positive, asking herself what lesson she was learning, what the higher purpose of it was. The lessons for her were to always look for positives, even in the face of adversity, to be patient and to listen to her body, because it is such a fantastic machine and it knows a lot more than the conscious mind could ever know.

Although it was a bumpy ride for a couple of years with a lowered immune system, she is now 100% fine and is planning her first child.

Whilst always a naturally positive person, she can get down and she has to remind herself of the power of positive thinking, that we choose our thoughts, and our thoughts create our experience of the world, and that in turn affects our bodies.

For a full version of this story, contact tricia@pw-hypnotherapy.co.uk.

LIST BELOW THE PEOPLE YOU FIND INSPIRING AND WHY:

Don't worry about the world coming to an end today.

It's already tomorrow in Australia.

Charles Schultz

The Ten Step Programme

This is a simple ten step programme to help you recognise your negative thoughts, see the consequences of them and lead the way to transforming them into thoughts which are constructive, helpful, encouraging and empowering. It is important to complete each and every one of these steps to derive the maximum benefit. There are a couple of completed examples for you so that you can see the process in action.

Step 1   **Identify the thought**

Make it as specific as possible rather than a generalisation. For example, it is better to say "I don't feel confident enough to go into work today" which is specific, rather than "I am not confident" which is general. In addition, "I am not confident" is a **belief**. Something which you believe to be true and act as though it was. This process is less effective when you work with beliefs. It is much better if you work with specific **thoughts**. Just to emphasise, beliefs are what you feel to be true, and act as though they **are** true. The thought may come from a belief but is much more specific to a situation. Here are some more examples to help you:

BELIEF	THOUGHT
I am not good enough	I can't go to that party – I haven't got anything to say to anyone
I am fat	I feel really fat today

Working on the thoughts will have a more immediate effect.

Step 2   **Identify the evidence for the thought**

Often our thoughts aren't really backed up with actual evidence, but whatever evidence there is can be listed here. For example, to the thought "I haven't got anything to say to anyone", your evidence might be "At the last party I went to I didn't say a word". List as many as you can.

Step 3 **Identify the evidence against the thought**

It is often the case that evidence against a thought far outweighs evidence for it but we rarely even think about it. Now's your chance to start challenging those little gremlins. Using the same example, evidence might be "I did speak with three people at the party before that one". List as many as you can.

Step 4 **Decide which of the thinking patterns it represents**

It is useful to start to look at what type of thinking you are adopting so that you can become more aware of it and see examples of alternative thinking patterns (pages 30-31). Go to the chapter on Thinking Patterns and see which style it most closely fits. Do you notice that you have a negative pattern you use more than any other?

Step 5 **Establish how the thought makes you feel**

What **feelings** does the negative thought engender within you? Usually these feelings will also be negative. Examples might be angry, sad, useless, powerless, used, ugly – you get the idea.

Step 6 **Determine whether there is a purpose to this thought which doesn't cause you stress**

This is worth repeating "Determine whether there is a purpose to this thought which **does not cause you stress**". Stress-free. I don't know of any negative thought that is also free from stress.

Step 7 **Reality/logic/perspective challenge**

This again is another way of challenging the negative thinking. Examples are as follows – choose whichever ones seem to fit your statement.

Reality check:
How do I know that thought is true?
Who says?
What's so bad about that?

Logic check:
How does this logically follow?
Is this based on fact or emotion?
How reasonable is this?

Perspective check:
What is the worst thing that could happen?
What are the odds of this happening?
How would the outside world view this situation?
What are the odds of this happening
What's the best that could happen?
What are the odds of this happening?

Step 8　**Come up with an alternative, positive thought**

I know, you haven't worked this muscle in a while! It may take a little bit of practice to start developing an alternative positive thought, and you don't have to completely believe it just yet. However, it is useful to ask yourself whether the new thought is:

a)　　More realistic
b)　　More logical
c)　　More likely

An example of a positive thought using the example above might be "I can talk about sport/my favourite hobby/their favourite hobby/the latest gossip/what's in the news" or "It's easy if I remember that it isn't a test and that it's just about getting to know people and having fun".

Step 9　**Establish how that thought makes you feel**

Chances are that the new positive thought will make you feel stronger, more confident, empowered – even if only marginally at first. Play around with the positive thought until you notice it making a positive difference on how you feel within yourself.

There are some circumstances where it is appropriate to feel some negative emotion, but it is of the healthy kind, and in proportion to the problem. For example "disappointment", "concern" or "sadness" may be appropriate and certainly preferable to "outrage", "anxious" or "devastated". If someone has let you down badly, it is appropriate to feel disappointed but not so much that it ruins your day. If you have been diagnosed with a life-threatening illness, it is appropriate to feel concern, but not the level of anxiety where it spoils your every waking moment – the concern should be sufficient that you are taking care of yourself and making the most of the life you do have. If a loved one has passed away, it is appropriate to feel devastated for a while but that should turn into sadness and then acceptance whilst you start to rebuild your life. For the most part this book is dealing with less significant negative situations for which you should certainly be seeking a positive emotion rather than a lesser negative one.

Step 10 **Decide whether you are now willing to let go of the negative thought**

Decision time. Now you know the benefits of the positive thought and the futility of the negative thought, are you ready and willing to let go of the old to accommodate the new? Now? If not, it may be that you need to do a little more work on the positive thought so it **feels** right, **sounds** right and **looks** right.

There are a couple of examples of this process in action to help guide you in Part II.

Be diligent. Be persistent. Practice makes perfect. Remember that this is a process not an event.

NOTE

If you have purchased this book as part of an email support programme, you may contact Tricia Woolfrey at tricia@pw-hypnotherapy.co.uk who will help you to come up with positive thoughts that make you feel good. You may also decide at this point to purchase email support by contacting her at the above email address.

Other Ideas

Here are some more ideas to help you overcome the negativity and develop a positive mental attitude. Choose the ones which appeal to you and practise them. Some will appeal more than others. And remember that sometimes those which appeal the least are actually the most helpful! Be discerning and be persistent!

1. **Thought Stopping**

   If you get a negative thought, simply say in a firm voice "Stop! Next!" and move on. You may find that you move to the same thought, or your thoughts move onto something else. Of course you are aiming for the latter, but if you find that you return to the same negative thought, simply repeat "Stop! Next". Your subconscious will soon get the message.

2. **Swap your Shoulds for Coulds**

   Many people live by what is called "The Tyranny of the Shoulds" - using words like "should", "must", "got to" and "have to". This can leave you feeling resentful, guilt-ridden or worse, disempowered. If you swap "should" for "could" or "choose" it completely changes how you feel about something, offering you choice and so it empowers you more.

3. **Think of Something Positive**:

   - A happy memory

   - Someone who loves you

   - Someone you love

   - The beauty of nature

   - An achievement you are proud of

It may be that the negative thought comes back. If this happens, simply bring yourself back to the same or another positive thought. Eventually the negative thought will disappear. Keep working that positive thinking muscle and it will become stronger each and every day as the negative one withers.

4.   **Find the Good**

Often negative thinking can come from our propensity to find what we don't like about something – focusing on the negative: "It was a lousy party – I didn't like the food". Instead, focus on the good, something you can appreciate and notice how it lifts your mood: "It was a good party – I met some interesting people". Maybe you didn't like the food but it doesn't have to colour your entire experience of the party!

5.   **Identify the Negative Influences in Your Life**

Do you have people in your life who are negative? How do you feel in their company? If they are a drain on your energy and influence you in a way which drags you down, limit the time you spend with them. Choose your friends wisely. And your music for that matter, and your reading choices, and your viewing choices. All media have an effect on your mood – if they don't help you feel good, stop doing them.

6.   **Have an Inner-Advisor**

This can be somebody you know, a famous person known for their positivity, creativity or wisdom or even a fictitious character. And you don't have to limit it to one either, you can have a whole board of inner-advisors who can coach you, depending on the context. You could have one for your relationships, another for situations where you need to be more assertive, another where you need someone who can give you confidence about your career, etc. Be creative! Consult your inner-advisors whenever you need to and, once you practise this technique, you will be able to benefit from their wisdom. It is a terrific way of accessing the creativity of your subconscious mind.

7.   **Let Negative Thoughts Float Away**

Imagine yourself blowing your negative thoughts into a balloon, tie it up nice and tight and watch it float away. Notice how much lighter you feel. You can use other visualisation techniques, ie see the negative thought written in the sand, then a wave comes in and wipes it away. Be creative!

8.   **Create Negative-Thinking Time**

Decide what time of day you would like to do all your negative thinking and for how long. For example, you may decide that you will do this for 10 minutes at 9.30 each morning. Or Fridays at 10. Write down any negative thoughts and put them together in a safe place. Revisit them at the appointed time. Then decide whether you want to bin it, solve it or keep it to think about again tomorrow.

9.   **Take Action**

If you are thinking about a problem - solve it or forget it (see The Serenity Prayer, following). Think of as many solutions to the problem as possible – whether the ideas make sense or not. Rank your ideas in order of feasibility, considering the resources and time available to you and whether there may be any negative consequences to the action which outweigh the benefits. Select the best idea and create an action plan to put it into place. Carry out each step and evaluate progress as you go, fine-tuning if necessary. Most plans, like a ship's course, need adjusting along the way. When you have achieved your goal, reward yourself – you deserve it!

10. **The Serenity Prayer**

The Serenity Prayer was thought to be written by Reinhold Niebuhr and encourages you to let go of those things over which you have no control. It is used by members of Alcoholics Anonymous but is helpful and relevant to most of us in our daily lives.

> Grant me the serenity to accept the things I cannot change
> Give me the courage to change the things I can
> And the wisdom to know the difference

If the situation is not something you can do anything about – accept it and move on. Dwelling on it solves nothing – and there are lots of positives to focus on!

11. **Identify new core beliefs**

Core beliefs are things that we believe are true that govern our behaviour and choices. Start by finishing these sentences using your first, gut reaction. It is best to use only one or two words for each:

■   I am ….

■   People are …

■   The world is …

This will identify your core beliefs. Are they positive or negative? In the introduction, Sarah had very negative core beliefs "I am not good enough"; "People are difficult"; "The world is tough". Clearly, these were creating a very negative experience for her. Once you have identified any negative core beliefs, transform them into something more positive. For Sarah these might be "I am capable"; "People are helpful"; "The world is exciting". These are just suggestions – use whatever works for you. Then, each day, gather evidence for your new core beliefs and log them in a journal. Make a note of as many as possible for as long as you need to. With time your subconscious mind will adopt the new positive core beliefs as a natural default pattern.

Let's look at how this might look for Sarah:

OLD CORE BELIEF		
I am not good enough	People are difficult	The world is tough
NEW CORE BELIEF		
I am capable	People are helpful	The world is exciting
EVIDENCE		
A customer said they were really happy with my work	My neighbour helped me move some furniture	I had an offer of a new job – more pay and a better company
I got that job offer	My brother gave me some good advice on my finances	My family arranged a surprise party for my birthday
My family complimented me on the Sunday lunch I organised – my first!	Katy is taking me shopping to help me find a new outfit for the wedding	I have been invited for a skiing holiday by a friend

And just keep going until you have fully embraced the new core beliefs.

12.   A Digital Vision Board

A digital vision board is a software program into which you can write your favourite positive affirmations and include inspirational pictures. It can be used as a screen saver as a way of keeping you positive and focused. Available from www.self-help-resources.co.uk.

13.   Bach Flower Remedies

Bach Flower Remedies are reputed to help you manage the ups and downs of everyday life and are widely available at health food shops. Either take two drops on the tongue or you can mix up to seven remedies by putting a couple of drops of each in water. Repeat as necessary. If you are pregnant please consult your doctor.

Here are the main ones for negativity: Beech is useful if you feel critical or intolerant towards others; Holly if you feel wounded, jealous or spiteful; Centaury is useful if you find it hard to say "no"; Walnut if you feel unsettled in times of change or are affected by a dominant personality; Aspen if you have anxiety without knowing the cause; Mimulus if you feel anxious about something specific; Rock Rose for extreme terror; Cherry Plum if you fear losing control; Honeysuckle if your mind is stuck in the past; White Chestnut if your mind is going round in circles; Mustard if you feel depressed and you don't know why; Impatients if you are impatient; Gentian for feeling discouraged after a setback; Gorse if you give up when things go wrong; Cerato if you know what to do but doubt your judgement or ability; Willow if you feel resentful and sorry for yourself; Pine for guilt and self-blame; Sweet Chestnut for extreme anguish; Larch for lack of confidence; Crab Apple if you dislike something about yourself.

14   **Change your Biochemistry**

Our moods are affected by levels of serotonin and endorphins. In order to boost serotonin, it is important to make sure you get sunlight when you can, eat protein with each meal, and eat the following foods – you might call them "Good Mood Foods": asparagus, banana, beef, broccoli, bamboo shoots, chicken, crab, crayfish, cod, Dover sole, duck, game, greens, kidney beans, kiwi, lamb, lobster, low fat cheddar cheese, mung beans, mushrooms (white or portabello) mussels, nigari, plums, pineapple, pork, prawns, red leaf lettuce, salmon, sesame seeds, skimmed milk, snapper, spinach, spirulina seaweed, soy sauce, sunflower seeds, tofu, tuna, turkey, veal.

In order to boost endorphins you need to eliminate sugars, take plenty of exercise, listen to relaxing or "feel good" music and spend time with people you love – including pets!

15.   **Meditation**

The defining characteristic of meditation is conscious breathing and, as a process, it is helpful in achieving health, wellbeing and a sense of inner peace. There are many forms of meditation and it is worthwhile finding out about classes near you. Dr Andrew Weil, a proponent of alternative medicine, says that "You cannot be upset if your breathing is slow, deep, quiet and regular."

16. **7th Path ® Self-Hypnosis**

This is a cross between meditation and self-hypnosis, plus some! Much more powerful than standard self-hypnosis, this is an excellent and powerful way of creating positive change in your life and for stopping those negative thoughts in a supportive way which develops you personally. You can create a sense of inner peace, increased motivation, self-esteem and positive thoughts. Courses are available. For information, see the Resources section in Part III.

YOUR IDEAS:

Thinking Patterns

These thinking patterns are based on the work by Dr David Burns, a proponent of cognitive behavioural therapy. He believes, as do many other prominent psychologists, that our thoughts affect our emotional state, and that negative thoughts lead to negative emotions and completely colour our experience of ourselves, of others and the world.

The word "cognitive" refers to our ability to think, learn and remember. So, how we process thought affects our perceptions, our perceptions affect our reality and our reality affects our experience of the world. By altering the way we look at things, the things we look at change.

We have approximately 2 million bits of data available to us at any one time. This is clearly too much for anyone to be able to process in any meaningful way. Add to this the dynamic that we can only hold in our conscious mind an average of 7 bits of data, this means there is an awful lot of culling to do. To make sense of the data, we filter it through our values, beliefs and life experiences. This causes us to distort it to fit in with our expectations, we delete data that we do not feel is relevant or that we don't want to know, or we generalise, ie people are always late/mean/thoughtless/selfish/kind, etc. The clue to a generalisation is that the word "always" or "never" is there. This filtering is why, if you have a number of people go through the same experience, they never (oops, there goes another generalisation!) describe it in the same way. Each person will use their own filters, will delete different things, distort in different ways and have alternative generalisations.

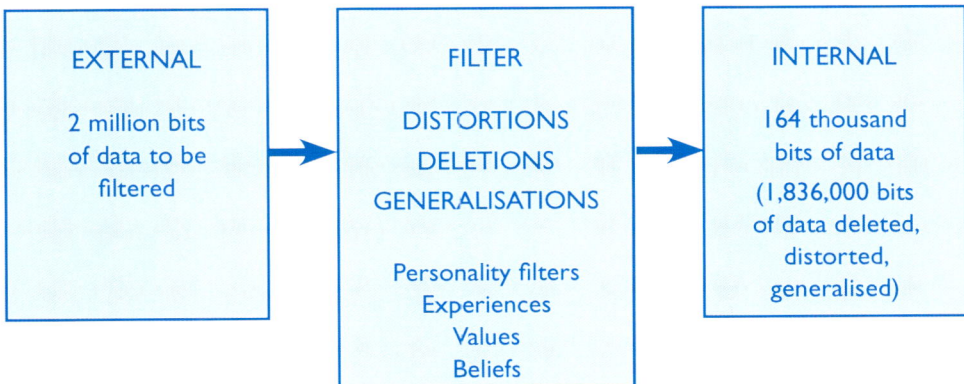

EXTERNAL	FILTER	INTERNAL
2 million bits of data to be filtered	DISTORTIONS DELETIONS GENERALISATIONS Personality filters Experiences Values Beliefs	164 thousand bits of data (1,836,000 bits of data deleted, distorted, generalised)

Let's take Laura, Adam and Jenny who go out to dinner.

Laura's story:

Adam, Jenny and I went out last night to a lovely restaurant which I hadn't been to before. An Italian. The service was brilliant and the food was very good too though I thought it was a little rich for me and I couldn't eat it all.

Adam's story:

The three of us went out again. It was another fraught evening with Laura and Jenny arguing about work. I don't know why we bother. It's always the same old problem every time.

Jenny's story:

We went out last night, the three of us. Adam was late. As usual. What is it with men? They always let you down. But, other than that, we had a great time. Laura and I talked a lot about the problems at work and it was good to get things off our chest.

They all were together at the same event yet, from their stories, there is very little to identify with. Laura was interested in the food and made no mention of any tension on the night. Adam just focused on the problems he saw between Jenny and Laura and Jenny felt irritated by Adam's lateness but otherwise that they had a good time and implied that the discussions were a way of them relieving the stresses of the day rather than causing the stresses of the evening.

Effectively, they were all filtering the information:

Deleting

Adam and Jenny didn't even mention the restaurant or the food and Laura didn't mention the discussions. These facts were deleted.

Distorting

Adam and Jenny had a completely different take on the discussions. Adam thought they were fraught whereas Jenny thought they were helpful.

Generalisations

Jenny generalised that men always let you down. The words "always" and "never" are clues as to whether it is a generalisation.

Experiences

They will each have life experiences which caused them to filter the information in their own way.

Values

Clearly Laura values good food, Adam values harmony, Jenny values having her time respected and being able to discuss problems.

Beliefs

Laura has the belief that to have a good time you have to have a good restaurant and good service. Adam has the belief that to have a good time you cannot talk about problems. On the other hand Jenny believes that to have a good time you need to talk through problems with someone who understands.

Why is it important to know all of this? Because our perceptions are only reality from our own perspective. Other people's realities can be different. We can choose our reality by the way we think and what we choose to focus on.

Focusing on what are wrong with things gives a feeling of constant dissatisfaction. Alternatively, to focus on the positive gives us a rosier perspective on life. You can choose which experience you want simply by choosing which of the 2 million bits of information you focus on!

Following is an adaptation of the distortions which Dr David Burns came up with. It lists the actual style with a description of it and an example of that thinking style. In the right-hand column you will see an alternative, positive thought which will help you to feel more positive.

STYLE	DESCRIPTION/EXAMPLE	ALTERNATIVE
All or nothing thinking	Everything is black or white – there are no shades of grey. ie She is really bad.	She is neither bad nor good, she is a little of both, as we all are.
Over generalisation	ie "He doesn't like me" means that nobody likes me.	He may or may not like me but other people do.
Mental filter	Dwelling on a negative detail. ie only noticing that your hair is a mess today.	So my hair is a mess today, I'm wearing my best outfit and I'm feeling good!
Disqualifying the positive	Deciding that any positive experience doesn't count. ie saying "I'm a mess" if someone compliments you on what you are wearing.	Thank you! (for the compliment).
Jumping to conclusions	Making a negative interpretation without the facts. ie "She doesn't think I'm doing a good job".	Ask yourself how you know this is true?
Magnification or Minimisation	Exaggerating or minimising the importance of things. ie "I've eaten a chocolate – I've blown it. I may as well forget the diet".	It's only one chocolate. More will make the problem worse. I haven't blown it unless I carry on eating more chocolate. I'm taking back control.
Emotional reasoning	Assuming that negative emotions reflect the way things really are. ie after a row with your partner, thinking that life isn't worth living anymore.	Just because I feel bad today doesn't make *life* bad.
"Should" statements	I must, have to, got to, should. ie "I should have more friends/more money/a better job/be married/lose weight/keep up with the Jones'".	What would happen if I didn't? Who said I should? Why? I can choose whether I want to or not.

Labelling and Mislabelling	An extreme form of generalisation. ie "I didn't get that promotion so I'm a total failure".	So I didn't get the promotion – I am still good at my job.
Personalisation	Thinking you are the cause of any event. ie "My son's in trouble and it's all my fault".	My son's in trouble because **he** did something wrong. He makes his own choices.
What If	Anticipating the worst outcome(s) to any event. ie "What if I make a mistake?"	Ask yourself "What if it all goes **well**? I can plan for any problems and I can still expect the best".

Nothing but your thoughts can make you think you are vulnerable.
A Course in Miracles

A Word About Words

In this book we have talked about the effect that thoughts have on our feelings. I wanted to let you know that this can also be true of individual words.

Let me explain: the brain is a highly sophisticated and complex tool. It regulates unconscious processes such as breathing, balance, heartbeat, digestion and survival instincts as well as allowing us to think and learn. It is responsible for associating, linking and connecting. It is also involved in our behaviour and emotions. Any word, smell, symbol, image, taste, sound, touch or emotion will be associated, linked or connected with something else so that you can make sense of it and these then can impact our emotions.

It is incredible to think that, whilst homo sapiens have been on this earth for millions of years, the location of the brain was only discovered some 500 years ago and scientists are **still** trying to understand its intricacies even now.

Negatives –v– positives

Despite its incredible sophistication, the brain does not process negatives well. For example, if you say to yourself "don't panic" the brain only really hears "panic". Since "don't" (do not) is a negative, it is ignored, thereby giving you an instruction to panic – the complete opposite of what you want.

Similarly, when you say to yourself "don't forget", the unconscious mind hears "forget", which is effectively an **instruction** to forget. Since what you really want to do is remember, t is much better to say to yourself "remember to …"

What you focus on you give energy to, so by focusing on panicking and forgetting, that is what you are getting.

Since the opposite of panic is calm, a better phrase to use over "don't panic" is "calm". A client of mine who had a fear of spiders constantly said "there's nothing to be scared of" as a way of reassuring herself. Of course, her brain was hearing "scared" and so her emotions complied!

she would have been better to say "I'm perfectly safe". There are very few exceptions to this rule so a general rule of thumb is to steer clear of focusing on what you want to avoid.

Will –v– am

If you are looking to create some kind of change in your life, such as to become tidier around the home, or more organised, it is a mistake to say "I will be tidier and more organised". The reason is that "will" places things in the future and, since the future is never the present, it means that it never happens. Much better to say "I **am** tidy and organised" which places it firmly in the "now" so that your brain can start organising itself around being tidy and, well, organised! You start to adopt new behaviours which create a new reality for you.

But –v– even though

Words can also create our experience. For example, the use of that simple word "but" can have a profound effect on us, as demonstrated below:

The flowers are beautiful **but** they will not last
The flowers are beautiful **and** they will not last
The flowers are beautiful **even though** they will not last

The use of the word "but" effectively negates the positive aspect of the flowers by focusing the mind of their impending doom. The use of the word "and" embraces their beauty and their vulnerability by giving both equal power. However, the use of the words "even though" focuses more on the positive and minimises the effect of the negative, so creating a more positive experience.

Let's try some more:

I have made it up with my partner **but** we may fall out again
I have made it up with my partner **and** we may fall out again
I have made it up with my partner **even though** we may fall out again

I am learning French **but** I find the grammar tricky
I am learning French **and** I find the grammar tricky
I am learning French **even though** I find the grammar tricky

Can you feel the difference? Hear the difference? See the difference?

What experience does each give you? What you are after is a more positive effect so that what you say to yourself enables you to feel good, or at least better.

These small adjustments completely impact how you feel.

Difficulty –v- ease

A client of mine who wanted to lose weight said to me "I would like to work as hard as possible so I don't eat junk". Those were her actual words. She had been a binge eater. She was programming herself that it would be "hard" and that she **would** "eat junk". Instead of saying that something will be "hard" or "difficult" use the word "ease". It would have had a much more positive effect for her to have said "eating healthy food will be easy". Or, "I'm losing weight easily and effortlessly". Focusing on ease is so much … easier!

Try –v– do

Lots of people talk about trying. The above client also used the phrase "try to lose weight". She was really setting herself up! "Try" is my least favourite word after "but". Basically, it is signaling to the mind that there will be a constant battle between the part of her which wants to lose weight and the part of her which wants to eat junk. "Try" is effort meeting resistance. The only "try" I would advocate is the "try" which involves sampling a new food, or to determine if some item of clothing or footwear fits and/or suits you. Otherwise, it is simply bad news. Much better to say "I **am** losing weight". **Trying** is not **doing.** Since what you want to **do** is lose weight, use an active adverb.

The Power of "Yet"

One of my favourite words is "yet". It is very powerful. Let me demonstrate. "I am learning to program computers but can't do it **yet**." "Yet" is a process word. It tells you that you can expect something in the future. However, like a superpower – it can be used for good or evil (empowerment or disempowerment)!

Empowerment - "I can't do that yet" presupposes that you will be able to do it at some point in the future. It gives hope and recognises that most things are a process and this is simply the early stages of that process.

Disempowerment - I haven't failed yet, implies that failure is imminent.

Better to say "It has worked so far" rather than simply taking "yet" off the sentence. This adjustment, whilst still open to the possibility of failure, focuses on the positive aspects of success and minimises the risk of failure.

Only/Just

The use of words such as "only" and "just" again can be used to empower or disempower:

Empowerment – For example, "It was only a small mistake" – minimises the effect of the mistake "It was just a little blip", again minimises the problem and any incumbent guilt around it.

Disempowerment – "I am only an administrator" – this is a real blow to your sense of self. Much better to say "I am an administrator". There is no "only" about it. If you don't value yourself, you will find it difficult to find others who will do that for you.

"I am just starting out" – whilst not as disempowering as the previous statement, it places you in a position of vulnerability at the bottom of a ladder. The message can be made more positively by simply leaving out the word "just", so that you have "I am starting out".

Words to Children

Another client of mine spoke of her dismay that her son was not settling into nursery. When I asked her what she said to him before he went into nursery, she said "It's only a few hours. I will be with you soon". This mum clearly doted on her son and wanted to reassure him. However her words, spoken with love, actually set him up to believe that nursery was something to be endured rather than enjoyed and that salvation would come soon in the form of his mother. It is no wonder that he was struggling. By focusing instead on what fun he will have and that the time will fly by, he can expect a much more positive experience.

Remember (note the choice of word!), simple adjustments can create big results.

> Be careful what you say to yourself,
> your mind is always listening!

PART II

EXAMPLE I

Step 1 – the negative thought – make it as specific as possible rather than a generalisation

I'll never get that job

Step 2 – what is the evidence for the thought?

They want someone with more experience than me
I haven't done that level of work before – How do I know I can?

Step 3 - what is the evidence against the thought? List as many as you can.

*I didn't know **this** job before I took it on and I do OK*
People often get jobs without meeting all the criteria the company is looking for
I'm a quick learner

Step 4 - which thinking pattern does the thought represent? (p32-33)

Jumping to conclusions

Step 5 - how does it make me feel?

Hopeless, useless, trapped, disempowered

Step 6 - is there a purpose to this thought which does not cause me stress?

Er, no, it just makes me feel stressed. This thought is doing me no good at all!

Step 7 - reality/logic/perspective challenge (p18-19)

I don't know the thought is true because the decision isn't mine, so the assumption is not reasonable. I also don't know the calibre of the other candidates. My statement is based on pure emotion. The worst thing that would happen is that I don't get the job - big deal - the practice will be good for me. I might not WANT the job after I have the interview. The odds of my not getting the job are about 50/50 – nothing ventured nothing gained. The outside world would view this as defeatist and that I should just go for it!

Step 8 - alternative positive thought

I will enjoy meeting with them to find out if I want the job and to show them how good an employee I am, the great experience I have and that I am a quick learner. I am interviewing them just as much as they are interviewing me - it needs to be right for both of us.

Step 9 - how does *that* make me feel?

Confident, in control, empowered, hopeful and positive

Step 10 - am I willing to let go of the negative thought? When?

Most definitely! And now!

Persons are judged to be great because of the positive qualities they possess, not because of the absence of faults.
Anon

EXAMPLE II

Step 1 – the negative thought – make it as specific as possible rather than a generalisation

I've had one biscuit. I've blown the diet. I may as well have the whole packet.

Step 2 – what is the evidence for the thought?

I just had a biscuit and I wasn't supposed to – I'm on a weight loss plan

---

Step 3 - what is the evidence against the thought? List as many as you can.

*I've only blown it if I carry on eating the biscuits. One biscuit does not put on weight.
A packet of biscuits does.*

Step 4 - which thinking pattern does the thought represent? (p32-33)

All or nothing, magnification

Step 5 - how does it make me feel?

Out of control, hopeless, fat

Step 6 - is there a purpose to this thought which does not cause me stress?

Not at all

Step 7 - reality/logic/perspective challenge (p18-19)
This isn't reasonable. Just because I ate one biscuit isn't a sign to pile on even more calories. If I stop here there is no damage. It doesn't logically follow that because I have one biscuit I have to have a packet – this is purely emotion driven and has no basis in fact. The outside world would view this situation that I now have a choice whether to take control or be out of control for a whole day – I choose the behaviour, I choose the consequence

Step 8 - alternative positive thought

I choose to stop now. I don't want any more

Step 9 - how does *that* make me feel?

Strong! In control!

Step 10 - am I willing to let go of the negative thought? When?

Now, if not sooner!

Remember, no one can make you feel inferior without your consent.
Eleanor Roosevelt

Step 1 – the negative thought – make it as specific as possible rather than a generalisation

Step 2 – what is the evidence for the thought?

Step 3 - what is the evidence against the thought? List as many as you can.

Step 4 - which thinking pattern does the thought represent? (p32-33)

Step 5 - how does it make me feel?

Step 6 - is there a purpose to this thought which does not cause me stress?

Step 7 - reality/logic/perspective challenge (p18-19)

Step 8 - alternative positive thought

Step 9 - how does *that* make me feel?

Step 10 - am I willing to let go of the negative thought? When?

There are always flowers for those who want to see them.
Henri Matisse

Example 4

Imagine you are starting a new job – a step up from your last job – and you feel it is a stretch for you. You never had much confidence anyway and, even though you have had lots of positive comments from your new supervisor about how well you are doing, you cannot help but have the negative thought "I'm dreading today, someone is going to find me out" (mental filter). This is clearly going to leave you scared, demotivated and anxiously awaiting your demise! A poor positive thought might be "Well, nobody's found me out yet!". This, whilst better than the negative thought, still has that feeling of impending doom about it. What would it be like to think instead "I wonder what I'm going to learn today?". This leaves you with a feeling of wonder and curiosity and suggests that every day is a learning opportunity and every day is an improvement on the day before, that you are in the process of continuous development (as we all are). Also, the thought "My supervisor has faith in me – and I'm getting better every day" will similarly leave you feeling happier.

Are these thoughts more realistic? More logical? More likely? I think so. Just try them on for size for a little while, play with them, see if you can make them even better.

Step 9 – how does *that* make me feel?

This is covered somewhat in the examples above. What you are looking for is a thought that leaves you feeling happier, more empowered, more hopeful. If it doesn't, you simply need to work on a more positive wording for your thought. Remember, you don't have to believe it yet.

Step 10 – am I willing to let go of the negative thought?

Well, did you decide to let go of the thought? Or did you decide to keep it? If the latter, why? What is the benefit of the thought?

Protection?

Does it protect you? Remember, you are no safer with negativity than you are without it. The only thing which can make you safer is to take action. Avoidance puts you into a weakened state and means that over time you simply cope less and less with life so that your world gets smaller and smaller so that you can feel safe. Remember the serenity prayer:

> Give me the serenity to accept the things I cannot change
>
> The courage to change the things I can
>
> And the wisdom to know the difference

If you can't change things, accept them, learn from them and move on.

The protective part of you needs to understand that in trying to protect you, it has actually been causing you more pain than real life would have given you. So perhaps that part would like to step back and allow you to manage your life yourself so that you can learn, grow and develop from life's experiences and it can help you when you really need it – when you are in real danger. It doesn't need to sweat the small stuff for you anymore.

As Helen Keller said, "Avoiding danger is no safer in the long run than outright exposure. The fearful are caught as often as the bold". It's just that the bold enjoy more happiness, a greater sense of achievement and wonder and excitement. That is what I call a good list!

Attention?

Does it get you attention? Attention is just a way for insecure people to feel loved. It isn't real love. I wonder what it would be like for you to feel loved and positive at the same time? Wow! If the only way you have of feeling loved is to get attention through your negativity, you need to learn to value yourself more so that others can value you. Or it could be that you have a co-dependent relationship where you need to be needy and your partner needs to "fix you" in order that you both feel good about yourselves. However, being a co-dependent means that your value depends on your willingness to devalue yourself. And you are worth more than that.

Perfection?

Perfection is largely a myth. It is not a human condition. It is simply something to strive for, it isn't an absolute. In fact, if your perfectionist streak is so strong that you need to look for all the negatives, you cannot enjoy all your achievements. And there are many. You learned to walk. You learned to talk. You learned to read. Those are significant achievements you made when you were very young. And there will have been many more. Take stock. Otherwise life becomes one long series of disappointments. And there isn't anything enjoyable or virtuous about that.

Know that:

- 80% is good enough
- that **you** are good enough
- that nothing is worth all the pain of the worrying
- that you can be successful, even if you make mistakes
- that you can be happy, even if you make mistakes
- that you can be happy and successful without worry

We tend to notice everybody else's positive points and we miss their negatives. By contrast, perfectionists notice all their negative points and miss their positives. That just doesn't make sense. Of course you will fall short – we all would! You have your own skills and attributes which make you who you are, uniquely you. And you can still work on improving them – with a sense of fun and achievement, not with a desperate, driving need.

NOW, are you willing to let go of that thought? You know it makes sense.

Step 1 – the negative thought – make it as specific as possible rather than a generalisation

Step 2 – what is the evidence for the thought?

Step 3 - what is the evidence against the thought? List as many as you can.

Step 4 - which thinking pattern does the thought represent? (p32-33)

Step 5 - how does it make me feel?

Step 6 - is there a purpose to this thought which does not cause me stress?

Step 7 - reality/logic/perspective challenge (p18-19)

Step 8 - alternative positive thought

Step 9 - how does *that* make me feel?

Step 10 - am I willing to let go of the negative thought? When?

Remember, no one can make you feel inferior without your consent.
Eleanor Roosevelt

Step 1 – the negative thought – make it as specific as possible rather than a generalisation

Step 2 – what is the evidence for the thought?

Step 3 - what is the evidence against the thought? List as many as you can.

Step 4 - which thinking pattern does the thought represent? (p32-33)

Step 5 - how does it make me feel?

Step 6 - is there a purpose to this thought which does not cause me stress?

Step 7 - reality/logic/perspective challenge (p18-19)

Step 8 - alternative positive thought

Step 9 - how does *that* make me feel?

Step 10 - am I willing to let go of the negative thought? When?

The pessimist sees difficulty in every opportunity. The optimist sees the opportunity in every difficulty.

Winston Churchill

Step 1 – the negative thought – make it as specific as possible rather than a generalisation

Step 2 – what is the evidence for the thought?

Step 3 - what is the evidence against the thought? List as many as you can.

Step 4 - which thinking pattern does the thought represent? (p32-33)

Step 5 - how does it make me feel?

Step 6 - is there a purpose to this thought which does not cause me stress?

Step 7 - reality/logic/perspective challenge (p18-19)

Step 8 - alternative positive thought

Step 9 - how does *that* make me feel?

Step 10 - am I willing to let go of the negative thought? When?

Once you replace negative thoughts with positive ones, you'll start having positive results.

Willie Nelson

Step 1 – the negative thought – make it as specific as possible rather than a generalisation

Step 2 – what is the evidence for the thought?

Step 3 - what is the evidence against the thought? List as many as you can.

Step 4 - which thinking pattern does the thought represent? (p32-33)

Step 5 - how does it make me feel?

Step 6 - is there a purpose to this thought which does not cause me stress?

Step 7 - reality/logic/perspective challenge (p18-19)

Step 8 - alternative positive thought

Step 9 - how does *that* make me feel?

Step 10 - am I willing to let go of the negative thought? When?

To be wronged is nothing unless you continue to
remember it.
Confucius

How Are You Doing Now?

Now you've had a little more practice, how is it going now? Is it getting easier?

As with everything, you may not get it right first time. Simply notice where you get stuck and look back again at the instructions. Reread the relevant sections and come back to it. Leave it 5 minutes if you have to. Take a breather, and come back to it. A fresh look may make all the difference.

Remember:

- Rome wasn't built in a day

- Jumpers weren't knitted with one stitch

- And a good wine is matured over time

This is a process, not an event. By sticking with it, you will reap rewards. The investment of your time will be repaid to you many times over. It is an investment, in you, in your wellbeing and in your life. Just keep on making those investments to earn the interest. Every penny counts!

As Winston Churchill famously said:

NEVER GIVE UP, NEVER GIVE UP, NEVER GIVE UP!

We all do better with practice. Diligence is key.

You may want to copy some of the motivational quotes and put them in conspicuous places to act as daily reminders.

Do whatever it takes. Your life will transform if you persist.

Remember, what we are doing here is developing your positive-thinking muscle. This is not a one-event process. It is a programme of daily repetitions which strengthen you. Athletes practise daily to be at the top of their game. Daily practice is required to be at the top of **your** game.

Step 1 – the negative thought – make it as specific as possible rather than a generalisation

Step 2 – what is the evidence for the thought?

Step 3 - what is the evidence against the thought? List as many as you can.

Step 4 - which thinking pattern does the thought represent? (p32-33)

Step 5 - how does it make me feel?

Step 6 - is there a purpose to this thought which does not cause me stress?

Step 7 - reality/logic/perspective challenge (p18-19)

Step 8 - alternative positive thought

Step 9 - how does *that* make me feel?

Step 10 - am I willing to let go of the negative thought? When?

Big shots are only little shots who keep shooting.
Christopher Morley

Step 1 – the negative thought – make it as specific as possible rather than a generalisation

Step 2 – what is the evidence for the thought?

Step 3 - what is the evidence against the thought? List as many as you can.

Step 4 - which thinking pattern does the thought represent? (p32-33)

Step 5 - how does it make me feel?

Step 6 - is there a purpose to this thought which does not cause me stress?

Step 7 - reality/logic/perspective challenge (p18-19)

Step 8 - alternative positive thought

Step 9 - how does *that* make me feel?

Step 10 - am I willing to let go of the negative thought? When?

He only profits from praise who values criticism.
Heinrich Heine

Step 1 – the negative thought – make it as specific as possible rather than a generalisation

Step 2 – what is the evidence for the thought?

Step 3 - what is the evidence against the thought? List as many as you can.

Step 4 - which thinking pattern does the thought represent? (p32-33)

Step 5 - how does it make me feel?

Step 6 - is there a purpose to this thought which does not cause me stress?

Step 7 - reality/logic/perspective challenge (p18-19)

Step 8 - alternative positive thought

Step 9 - how does *that* make me feel?

Step 10 - am I willing to let go of the negative thought? When?

Attitudes are contagious. Are yours worth catching?
Dennis and Wendy Mannering

Step 1 – the negative thought – make it as specific as possible rather than a generalisation

Step 2 – what is the evidence for the thought?

Step 3 - what is the evidence against the thought? List as many as you can.

Step 4 - which thinking pattern does the thought represent? (p32-33)

Step 5 - how does it make me feel?

Step 6 - is there a purpose to this thought which does not cause me stress?

Step 7 - reality/logic/perspective challenge (p18-19)

Step 8 - alternative positive thought

Step 9 - how does *that* make me feel?

Step 10 - am I willing to let go of the negative thought? **When?**

Wherever you go, no matter what the weather, always bring your
own sunshine.

Anthony J D'Angelo

Step 1 – the negative thought – make it as specific as possible rather than a generalisation

Step 2 – what is the evidence for the thought?

Step 3 - what is the evidence against the thought? List as many as you can.

Step 4 - which thinking pattern does the thought represent? (p32-33)

Step 5 - how does it make me feel?

Step 6 - is there a purpose to this thought which does not cause me stress?

Step 7 - reality/logic/perspective challenge (p18-19)

Step 8 - alternative positive thought

Step 9 - how does _that_ make me feel?

Step 10 - am I willing to let go of the negative thought? When?

If you don't get everything you want,
think of the things you don't want that you don't get.
Oscar Wilde

Step 1 – the negative thought – make it as specific as possible rather than a generalisation

Step 2 – what is the evidence for the thought?

Step 3 - what is the evidence against the thought? List as many as you can.

Step 4 - which thinking pattern does the thought represent? (p32-33)

Step 5 - how does it make me feel?

Step 6 - is there a purpose to this thought which does not cause me stress?

Step 7 - reality/logic/perspective challenge (p18-19)

Step 8 - alternative positive thought

Step 9 - how does *that* make me feel?

Step 10 - am I willing to let go of the negative thought? When?

Positive thinking will let you do everything better
than negative thinking will.
Zig Ziglar

Step 1 – the negative thought – make it as specific as possible rather than a generalisation

Step 2 – what is the evidence for the thought?

Step 3 - what is the evidence against the thought? List as many as you can.

Step 4 - which thinking pattern does the thought represent? (p32-33)

Step 5 - how does it make me feel?

Step 6 - is there a purpose to this thought which does not cause me stress?

Step 7 - reality/logic/perspective challenge (p18-19)

Step 8 - alternative positive thought

Step 9 - how does *that* make me feel?

Step 10 - am I willing to let go of the negative thought? When?

I had the blues because I had no shoes
until upon the street
I met a man who had no feet.
Ancient Persian Saying

Step 1 – the negative thought – make it as specific as possible rather than a generalisation

Step 2 – what is the evidence for the thought?

Step 3 - what is the evidence against the thought? List as many as you can.

Step 4 - which thinking pattern does the thought represent? (p32-33)

Step 5 - how does it make me feel?

Step 6 - is there a purpose to this thought which does not cause me stress?

Step 7 - reality/logic/perspective challenge (p18-19)

Step 8 - alternative positive thought

Step 9 - how does *that* make me feel?

Step 10 - am I willing to let go of the negative thought? When?

Lucky people see the positive side to their bad luck.
Richard Wiseman

Step 1 – the negative thought – make it as specific as possible rather than a generalisation

Step 2 – what is the evidence for the thought?

Step 3 - what is the evidence against the thought? List as many as you can.

Step 4 - which thinking pattern does the thought represent? (p32-33)

Step 5 - how does it make me feel?

Step 6 - is there a purpose to this thought which does not cause me stress?

Step 7 - reality/logic/perspective challenge (p18-19)

Step 8 - alternative positive thought

Step 9 - how does _that_ make me feel?

Step 10 - am I willing to let go of the negative thought? When?

It's so hard when I have to, and so easy when I want to.
Annie Gottlier

Step 1 – the negative thought – make it as specific as possible rather than a generalisation

Step 2 – what is the evidence for the thought?

Step 3 - what is the evidence against the thought? List as many as you can.

Step 4 - which thinking pattern does the thought represent? (p32-33)

Step 5 - how does it make me feel?

Step 6 - is there a purpose to this thought which does not cause me stress?

Step 7 - reality/logic/perspective challenge (p18-19)

Step 8 - alternative positive thought

Step 9 - how does *that* make me feel?

Step 10 - am I willing to let go of the negative thought? When?

Oh my friend, it's not what they take away from you that counts. It's what you do with what you have left.

Hubert Humphrey

Step 1 – the negative thought – make it as specific as possible rather than a generalisation

Step 2 – what is the evidence for the thought?

Step 3 - what is the evidence against the thought? List as many as you can.

Step 4 - which thinking pattern does the thought represent? (p32-33)

Step 5 - how does it make me feel?

Step 6 - is there a purpose to this thought which does not cause me stress?

Step 7 - reality/logic/perspective challenge (p18-19)

Step 8 - alternative positive thought

Step 9 - how does *that* make me feel?

Step 10 - am I willing to let go of the negative thought? When?

I've been through some terrible things in my life and
some of them actually happened.
Mark Twain

Step 1 – the negative thought – make it as specific as possible rather than a generalisation

Step 2 – what is the evidence for the thought?

Step 3 - what is the evidence against the thought? List as many as you can.

Step 4 - which thinking pattern does the thought represent? (p32-33)

Step 5 - how does it make me feel?

Step 6 - is there a purpose to this thought which does not cause me stress?

Step 7 - reality/logic/perspective challenge (p18-19)

Step 8 - alternative positive thought

Step 9 - how does *that* make me feel?

Step 10 - am I willing to let go of the negative thought? When?

Every day may not be good, but there's something
good in every day.
Unknown

Step 1 – the negative thought – make it as specific as possible rather than a generalisation

Step 2 – what is the evidence for the thought?

Step 3 - what is the evidence against the thought? List as many as you can.

Step 4 - which thinking pattern does the thought represent? (p32-33)

Step 5 - how does it make me feel?

Step 6 - is there a purpose to this thought which does not cause me stress?

Step 7 - reality/logic/perspective challenge (p18-19)

Step 8 - alternative positive thought

Step 9 - how does *that* make me feel?

Step 10 - am I willing to let go of the negative thought? When?

> To be interested in the changing seasons is a happier
> state of mind than to be hopelessly in
> love with spring.
> *George Santayana*

Step 1 – the negative thought – make it as specific as possible rather than a generalisation

Step 2 – what is the evidence for the thought?

Step 3 - what is the evidence against the thought? List as many as you can.

Step 4 - which thinking pattern does the thought represent? (p32-33)

Step 5 - how does it make me feel?

Step 6 - is there a purpose to this thought which does not cause me stress?

Step 7 - reality/logic/perspective challenge (p18-19)

Step 8 - alternative positive thought

Step 9 - how does *that* make me feel?

Step 10 - am I willing to let go of the negative thought? When?

Happiness is an attitude. We either make ourselves
miserable, or happy and strong. The amount
of work is the same.
Francesca Reigler

Step 1 – the negative thought – make it as specific as possible rather than a generalisation

Step 2 – what is the evidence for the thought?

Step 3 - what is the evidence against the thought? List as many as you can.

Step 4 - which thinking pattern does the thought represent? (p32-33)

Step 5 - how does it make me feel?

Step 6 - is there a purpose to this thought which does not cause me stress?

Step 7 - reality/logic/perspective challenge (p18-19)

Step 8 - alternative positive thought

Step 9 - how does *that* make me feel?

Step 10 - am I willing to let go of the negative thought? When?

If you don't like something change it; if you
can't change it, change the way
you think about it.
Mary Engelbreit

Step 1 – the negative thought – make it as specific as possible rather than a generalisation

Step 2 – what is the evidence for the thought?

Step 3 - what is the evidence against the thought? List as many as you can.

Step 4 - which thinking pattern does the thought represent? (p32-33)

Step 5 - how does it make me feel?

Step 6 - is there a purpose to this thought which does not cause me stress?

Step 7 - reality/logic/perspective challenge (p18-19)

Step 8 - alternative positive thought

Step 9 - how does *that* make me feel?

Step 10 - am I willing to let go of the negative thought? When?

So often times it happens that we live our lives
in chains, and we never even know
we have the key.
The Eagles "Already Gone"

Step 1 – the negative thought – make it as specific as possible rather than a generalisation

Step 2 – what is the evidence for the thought?

Step 3 - what is the evidence against the thought? List as many as you can.

Step 4 - which thinking pattern does the thought represent? (p32-33)

Step 5 - how does it make me feel?

Step 6 - is there a purpose to this thought which does not cause me stress?

Step 7 - reality/logic/perspective challenge (p18-19)

Step 8 - alternative positive thought

Step 9 - how does *that* make me feel?

Step 10 - am I willing to let go of the negative thought? When?

I don't think of all the misery but of the beauty
that still remains.
Anne Frank

Step 1 – the negative thought – make it as specific as possible rather than a generalisation

Step 2 – what is the evidence for the thought?

Step 3 - what is the evidence against the thought? List as many as you can.

Step 4 - which thinking pattern does the thought represent? (p32-33)

Step 5 - how does it make me feel?

Step 6 - is there a purpose to this thought which does not cause me stress?

Step 7 - reality/logic/perspective challenge (p18-19)

Step 8 - alternative positive thought

Step 9 - how does *that* make me feel?

Step 10 - am I willing to let go of the negative thought? When?

Every thought is a seed. If you plant crab apples,
don't count on harvesting
Golden Delicious.
Bill Meyer

Step 1 – the negative thought – make it as specific as possible rather than a generalisation

Step 2 – what is the evidence for the thought?

Step 3 - what is the evidence against the thought? List as many as you can.

Step 4 - which thinking pattern does the thought represent? (p32-33)

Step 5 - how does it make me feel?

Step 6 - is there a purpose to this thought which does not cause me stress?

Step 7 - reality/logic/perspective challenge (p18-19)

Step 8 - alternative positive thought

Step 9 - how does *that* make me feel?

Step 10 - am I willing to let go of the negative thought? When?

We are all in the gutter, but some of us are
looking at the stars.
Oscar Wilde

Step 1 – the negative thought – make it as specific as possible rather than a generalisation

Step 2 – what is the evidence for the thought?

Step 3 - what is the evidence against the thought? List as many as you can.

Step 4 - which thinking pattern does the thought represent? (p32-33)

Step 5 - how does it make me feel?

Step 6 - is there a purpose to this thought which does not cause me stress?

Step 7 - reality/logic/perspective challenge (p18-19)

Step 8 - alternative positive thought

Step 9 - how does *that* make me feel?

Step 10 - am I willing to let go of the negative thought? When?

To be upset over what you don't have is to waste
what you do have.
Ken S Keyes Jnr

Step 1 – the negative thought – make it as specific as possible rather than a generalisation

Step 2 – what is the evidence for the thought?

Step 3 - what is the evidence against the thought? List as many as you can.

Step 4 - which thinking pattern does the thought represent? (p32-33)

Step 5 - how does it make me feel?

Step 6 - is there a purpose to this thought which does not cause me stress?

Step 7 - reality/logic/perspective challenge (p18-19)

Step 8 - alternative positive thought

Step 9 - how does *that* make me feel?

Step 10 - am I willing to let go of the negative thought? When?

The only disability in life is a bad attitude.
Scott Hamilton

Step 1 – the negative thought – make it as specific as possible rather than a generalisation

Step 2 – what is the evidence for the thought?

Step 3 - what is the evidence against the thought? List as many as you can.

Step 4 - which thinking pattern does the thought represent? (p32-33)

Step 5 - how does it make me feel?

Step 6 - is there a purpose to this thought which does not cause me stress?

Step 7 - reality/logic/perspective challenge (p18-19)

Step 8 - alternative positive thought

Step 9 - how does *that* make me feel?

Step 10 - am I willing to let go of the negative thought? When?

If you aren't fired with enthusiasm,
you'll be fired with enthusiasm.
Vince Lombardi

Step 1 – the negative thought – make it as specific as possible rather than a generalisation

Step 2 – what is the evidence for the thought?

Step 3 - what is the evidence against the thought? List as many as you can.

Step 4 - which thinking pattern does the thought represent? (p32-33)

Step 5 - how does it make me feel?

Step 6 - is there a purpose to this thought which does not cause me stress?

Step 7 - reality/logic/perspective challenge (p18-19)

Step 8 - alternative positive thought

Step 9 - how does *that* make me feel?

Step 10 - am I willing to let go of the negative thought? When?

My riches consist not in the extent of my possessions,

but in the fewness of my wants.

J Brotherton

Step 1 – the negative thought – make it as specific as possible rather than a generalisation

Step 2 – what is the evidence for the thought?

Step 3 - what is the evidence against the thought? List as many as you can.

Step 4 - which thinking pattern does the thought represent? (p32-33)

Step 5 - how does it make me feel?

Step 6 - is there a purpose to this thought which does not cause me stress?

Step 7 - reality/logic/perspective challenge (p18-19)

Step 8 - alternative positive thought

Step 9 - how does *that* make me feel?

Step 10 - am I willing to let go of the negative thought? When?

I don't like that man. I must get to know him better.
Abraham Lincoln

Step 1 – the negative thought – make it as specific as possible rather than a generalisation

Step 2 – what is the evidence for the thought?

Step 3 - what is the evidence against the thought? List as many as you can.

Step 4 - which thinking pattern does the thought represent? (p32-33)

Step 5 - how does it make me feel?

Step 6 - is there a purpose to this thought which does not cause me stress?

Step 7 - reality/logic/perspective challenge (p18-19)

Step 8 - alternative positive thought

Step 9 - how does *that* make me feel?

Step 10 - am I willing to let go of the negative thought? When?

In the depth of winter I finally learned that there
was within me an invincible summer.
Albert Camus

PART III

Beyond the Power of Positive Thought

By the time you get to this page, you should have had sufficient practice that your thinking is now naturally positive. If you haven't you need to continue with the method until positive thinking is your natural default.

You were given free will. Will it!

Now you are ready for the next step which is about The Law of Attraction. There are many books written about this, some of which are mentioned in the Resources section. I would recommend that you devour them and read them regularly. Get audio versions if you learn more easily that way! Or both! Whatever it takes!

In the meantime, I will give you a brief outline here to get you started.

The Law of Attraction is basically the principal that what you think about you bring about. If you think you are poor, you attract poverty in your life. If you think you are lousy in relationships, you attract unsupportive relationships. If you think you are unhealthy, you attract illness. If you think you are a failure, you attract disappointment. It sounds simple. It is.

So my challenge to you is:

- Focus on health, not illness
- Focus on abundance, not lack
- Focus on what you want, not what you don't
- Focus on love and friendship, not sleights and resentments
- Focus on giving and receiving, not taking and hoarding
- Focus on tolerance, not judgment
- Focus on peace, not conflict or stress

You get the idea. Remember, that which you think about, you bring about. In addition, make a daily routine of thanking the Universe for your health, prosperity, happiness, all the love in your life and anything else you want. If you do this daily, investing emotion into it, it becomes a hypnotic suggestion which creates a vibration in the world attracting those things to you. You really need that emotional investment to create what you want. Mere repetition doesn't hack it.

Do everything with the spirit of focused intent – this creates focussed action. With repetition and emotional investment, skepticism can be transformed into belief and belief into reality.

The more you use this technique, the stronger it will come and you can create your own life template and fill it with whatever you want in your life.

Be an inspiration to those around you.

A quitter never wins. A winner never quits.
Napoleon Hill

Resources

Books and CDs

Loving What Is by Byron Katie
Don't Sweat the Small Stuff by Richard Carlson
Mind Over Mood by Dennis Greenberger PhD and Christine A Padesky PhD
Feel the Fear and Do it Anyway by Susan Jeffers
Eating, Drinking, Over-thinking by Dr Susan Nolen-Hoeksema
The Secret by Rhonda Byrne
Think and Grow Rich by Napoleon Hill *(don't be put off by the title)*
Man's Search for Meaning by Victor Frankl
The Luck Factor by Richard Wiseman
21 Ways and 21 Days to the Life You Want by Tricia Woolfrey
Confidence for the Life You Want by Tricia Woolfrey

7th Path ® Self-Hypnosis

Tricia Woolfrey runs 7th Path ® Self-Hypnosis workshops. Much more powerful than standard self-hypnosis, this is a holistic, mind-body-spirit approach to making powerful, positive changes in your life which will allow you to enjoy:

- Positive change
- An end to negative thinking
- Increased motivation
- Improved self-esteem
- Emotional healing
- Inner peace
- Freedom from fear
- And much, much more

For more information, visit www.pw-hypnotherapy.co.uk or contact info@pw-hypnotherapy.co.uk.

Coaching

Tricia Woolfrey can offer telephone coaching and/or 1:1 therapy at either Harley Street or Surrey. For more information, contact her on 0845 130 0854.

And Last But Not Least

- Positive friends and family
- Uplifting music
- Feel good films and TV
- All the skills and attributes that brought you to where you are now and caused you to decide to buy this book
- Your free will — the power to choose your thoughts and change your mood

Whether you think you can or think you can't,
either way you are right.
Henry Ford

Conclusion

Negative thinking is simply a bad habit. And habits can be changed. All it needs is your willing co-operation and determination to succeed. Oh, and practice too! Because we all do everything better with practice.

The process I have outlined is simple. However, it is not necessarily easy. It does require your ruthless determination to put to sleep once and for all the beast of negative thought.

What will you lose?

- Your low energy
- Being a drain on the people around you
- Noticing how people scurry away when they see you arrive
- A sense of inner turmoil and/or helplessness
- A feeling of dread and doom
- A belief that the glass is not just half empty but we are all dying of thirst! And FAST!
- An inability to enjoy anything because you never know what might go wrong

Then, and only then, can you enjoy all the wonderful benefits which belong to every optimist on the planet. What are these?

- A feeling that, no matter what happens in life, life is GOOD
- A knowing that, no matter what happens in life, there is a positive reason for it – a learning, or something better on the horizon
- A sense of inner peace
- A belief that, not only is the glass half full, but that there is plenty to go around
- A feeling of empowerment, that you can do anything you set your mind to
- Being fun to be around
- People seeking out your company
- Being able to have fun, even if, and because, things go wrong sometimes

I know - it's a trade-off. When you balance out what you will lose with what you will gain, it seems like a tough choice! And in truth, that's what it is. A choice. Your choice. Your life.

So, are you ready? Ready to Live, Laugh and Learn?

You have many resources to help you.

Enjoy each moment. You deserve nothing less.

I just want to share with you one more thought. I was sent this by my mother – an eternal optimist, who works as a PA in London despite being in her 70s. She sent me this from an unknown source but it sums life up beautifully:

Life should not be a journey to the grave with the intention of arriving safely in an attractive and well-preserved body but rather to skid sideways, champagne in one hand, strawberries in the other, body thoroughly used up, totally worn out and screaming…

"WOO HOO – WHAT A RIDE!"

About the Author

Tricia Woolfrey MNLP, DHP, MAPHP, FCIPD is an advanced clinical hypnotherapist, trainer and coach with practices in Harley Street and Surrey. Whilst the bulk of her work is in private practice, with a background in Human Resources, she occasionally undertakes work in the corporate world. Her passion is helping people realise their potential to get more from life, relationships and career. She works in a wide variety of areas including self-esteem, conflict management, anger management, stress management, assertiveness, business coaching and wellbeing, including a weight loss programme called The Only Weigh®. She balances the practical with a mind-body-spirit approach to help bring a sense of personal mastery to her clients.

She runs numerous workshops for personal development, self-hypnosis and weight management and has a range of CDs available as well as inspirational products. For more information visit www.pw-hypnotherapy.co.uk.

She regularly writes for and appears in national and local press and does regular talks.

If you would like to know more about her latest projects, visit her website www.pw-hypnotherapy.co.uk and sister website www.self-help-resources.co.uk.

She is married and lives in Surrey.

> **What you think about**
> **What you feel about**
> **What you do about**
> **Is what comes about**
> *Calvin D Banyan*